ABORIGINAL BIOGRAPHIES

Athletes

ANITA YASUDA

Weigl

Published by Weigl Educational Publishers Limited
6325 10th Street SE
Calgary, Alberta T2H 2Z9
Website: www.weigl.ca

Library and Archives Canada Cataloguing in Publication

Yasuda, Anita
     Athletes / Anita Yasuda.

(Canadian Aboriginal biographies)
Includes index.
ISBN 978-1-77071-455-7 (bound).—ISBN 978-1-77071-459-5 (pbk.)

        1. Indian athletes—Canada—Biography—Juvenile literature.
2. Native athletes—Canada—Biography—Juvenile literature.
3. Indians of North America—Canada—Sports—Juvenile literature.
I. Title. II. Series: Canadian Aboriginal biographies

GV697.A1Y37 2012   j796.092'271   C2011-908195-4

Printed in the United States of America in North Mankato, Minnesota
1 2 3 4 5 6 7 8 9 0 16 15 14 13 12

082012
WEP250612

Senior Editor: Heather Kissock
Art Director: Terry Paulhus

Every reasonable effort has been made to trace ownership and to obtain permission to reprint copyright material.

The publishers would be pleased to have any errors or omissions brought to their attention so that they may be corrected in subsequent printings.

We gratefully acknowledge the financial support of the Government of Canada through the Canada Book Fund for our publishing activities.

CONTENTS

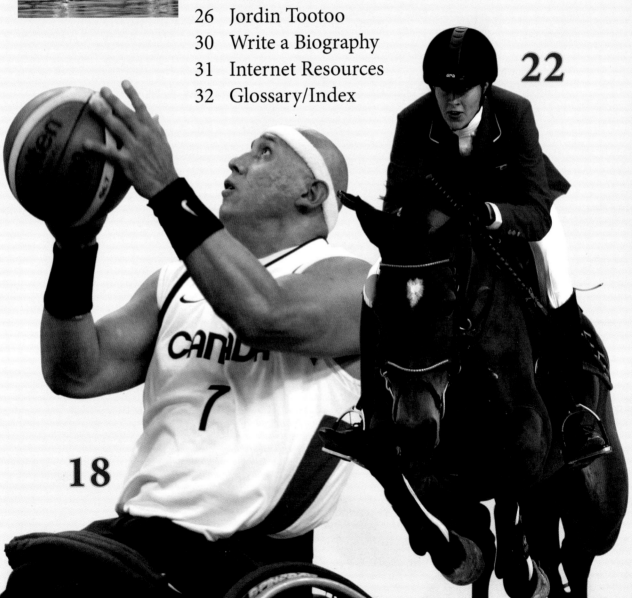

22

18

Introduction

Aboriginal athletes have played an important role in the history of Canadian sports. Some of their achievements took place many years ago, while other feats are more recent. In the early 1900s, for instance, Tom Longboat was one of the top **marathon** runners in the world. Angela Chalmers, on the other hand, won a bronze medal running in the 3,000-metre race at the 1992 **Olympic Games**. Before they retired, Bryan Trottier and Ted Nolan were well-known players in the National Hockey League. Skier Sammy Keny, hockey player Leah Sulyma, and Mareck Beaudoin, who competes in the **biathlon**, are a few of the Aboriginal athletes who are having success today. Through their dedication and hard work, these athletes have become role models for a new generation of Aboriginal athletes.

JORDIN TOOTOO

Canadian Aboriginal athletes may face a number of problems on their road to success. They sometimes do not have enough money or opportunity, and they often need help from their family, friends, teachers, and coaches. They sometimes get funding from companies and government groups, but it is often difficult for them to find enough financial support.

Aboriginal Peoples have organized their own sporting events to create opportunities for Aboriginal athletes. The Northern Games, the North American **Indigenous** Games, and the Arctic Sports Circle are some of these events. Programs such as the First Nations Snowboard Team help athletes develop their skills.

Tom Longboat, Colette Bourgonje, Alwyn Morris, Richard Peter, Monica Pinette, and Jordin Tootoo are Aboriginal athletes who represent excellence. They have blazed trails to compete in their sports. Some take part in well-known sports, while others compete in sports that do not receive much attention. These athletes have different skills and backgrounds, but they all have worked hard to reach their dreams.

TOM LONGBOAT

ALWYN MORRIS (RIGHT)

MONICA PINETTE

COLETTE BOURGONJE

RICHARD PETER

Long-Distance Runner
Tom Longboat

Tom Longboat was one of Canada's best long-distance runners. He began competing when he was still in his teens. In 1907, he became known around the world when he won the Boston Marathon, a long-distance race that attracts many top runners. His time in the race beat the previous record by almost five minutes. Longboat helped make marathon running a popular international sport. In his career, he won many races in North America and Europe, as well as representing Canada at the 1908 Olympics. In 1909, in one of Longboat's most memorable races, he was declared the Professional Champion of the World when he beat another great runner, Alf Shrubb of Great Britain,

Several trophies were awarded to Longboat during his career. Today, winners of the Tom Longboat Award have their names engraved on the Tom Longboat Trophy. This trophy is on display at the Canadian Sports Hall of Fame.

Personal Profile

in a marathon in New York City. It had looked as if Shrubb would win the race, but Longboat sped past him with only 3 kilometres left in the event.

Early Years

Thomas Charles Longboat was born in 1887. He was an Onondaga, one of the Six Nations that make up the **Iroquois Confederacy**. His Iroquois name, Cogwagee, means "everything." Longboat's family did not have much money. They had to work hard on their small farm. Longboat helped out, but he also found time to play **lacrosse** and race his brother around the countryside. When he was five, his father, George, died. Longboat had to help his mother, Betsey, by working on the farm and watching his brother.

Longboat went to school on the Six Nations **reserve**, although he often did not attend, as he was needed on the farm. When he was 12, he was sent to the Mohawk Institute, a school run by the Anglican Church. The government

> **"You've got to get out and run and stick through to the end to win."**

policy at the time was to educate Aboriginal children in church-run boarding schools where they would be forced to speak only English rather than their own language. Longboat was unhappy at the school, so he ran away and went back to the reserve.

Longboat began to enter races during his teenage years. In 1905, at the age of 17, he ran an 8-kilometre Victoria Day race in Caledonia, Ontario. Longboat did not win, but he came in second. This good finish encouraged him to train harder.

Longboat was known for his exceptional sprints toward the finish line at the end of races.

BORN Tom Longboat was born on June 4, 1887, on the Six Nations reserve near Brantford, Ontario.

FAMILY When Longboat was five years old, his father died. He grew up with his mother, two sisters, and one brother. Later, Longboat married Martha Silversmith. The couple had four children, three sons and one daughter.

EDUCATION Longboat attended school on the reserve. He briefly attended the Mohawk Institute until he ran away, unhappy that the school wanted him to drop his traditional ways.

CAREER Longboat competed in many marathons and other long-distance races. He served in the Canadian Armed Forces in World War I.

"I've had my day, no regrets."

Developing Skills

Longboat began to spend a great deal of time training. He ran all over the Six Nations reserve and to nearby towns. Once, he raced against a relative who was driving a horse and buggy. He still beat him.

In 1906, Longboat competed in his second Victoria Day race. This time, he won. Another Six Nations athlete named Bill Davis saw Longboat run. Davis, who had placed second in the 1901 Boston Marathon, encouraged Longboat to keep training. Longboat began to win many races in Canada.

One of them was the Around the Bay Road Race in Hamilton, Ontario, which is the oldest road race in North America. In 1907, Longboat went to

Longboat was one of the approximately 4,000 Canadian Aboriginals who served in World War I.

the United States, where he won the Boston Marathon, a 42.2-kilometre race. When he returned to Canada, Longboat was given a parade in Toronto. More than 200,000 people turned out to cheer for him.

The Path to Success

While preparing for the Boston Marathon, Longboat trained at a YMCA in Toronto. He would train very hard and then rest by taking long walks. The coaches at the YMCA did not approve of his methods. Reporters called him lazy and often used negative **stereotypes** to describe him.

In 1908, Longboat went to the Olympics in London, the capital of Great Britain. He was the favourite to win the marathon. The day of the race was very hot, and many of the runners fainted. About 30 kilometres into the race, when Longboat was in second place, he suddenly collapsed and could not finish the race. Many people thought that his career was over, but Longboat did not give up. Instead, he continued to train. He began to win again and defeated some of the best marathon racers in the world.

In 1916, Longboat joined the Canadian Armed Forces to fight in World War I. He was assigned to the 107th Pioneer Battalion in France, with the dangerous job of carrying messages and orders between units. He was wounded twice. In 1919, he returned to Canada. He farmed, worked in factories and steel mills, and was employed by the Toronto street cleaning department. He died of pneumonia in 1949 on the Six Nations reserve.

In 1951, the **Aboriginal Sport Circle** created the Tom Longboat Awards. They are given each year to the top male and female Aboriginal athletes in Canada. Longboat was also inducted into the Canadian Sports Hall of Fame and into the Canadian Indian Hall of Fame. Each year on June 4, Ontario celebrates Tom Longboat Day.

Accomplishments

1906 Longboat wins the Around the Bay Road Race in Hamilton, Ontario. He is almost three minutes ahead of the next-closest runner.

1907 Longboat wins the Boston Marathon in Boston, Massachusetts.

1907 Longboat wins the Ward's Island Marathon in Toronto, Ontario.

1908 Longboat again wins the Ward's Island Marathon.

1909 He is named the Professional Champion of the World after winning a marathon in New York City.

1912 Longboat sets a new 24-kilometre world record of 1 hour, 18 minutes, and 10 seconds during a race held in Edinburgh, Scotland.

1916 He serves in World War I with the 107th Pioneer Battalion, fighting in France.

Paralympic Racer
Colette Bourgonje

C olette Bourgonje is a remarkable athlete who is known for her determination and spirit. She has won many national and international racing and skiing championships for athletes with physical disabilities. Bourgonje burst onto the wheelchair racing scene in 1992 at the Paralympic Summer Games in Barcelona, Spain. The Paralympic Games, which take place soon after the Olympics, feature athletes with physical disabilities. Between 1992 and 2010, Bourgonje competed in nine Paralympic Games, where she won 10 medals. At the 2010 Paralympic Winter Games, which were held in Vancouver, British Columbia, Bourgonje won a silver medal and a bronze medal in **sit-ski** events. She became the first Canadian

Personal Profile

Bourgonje is no stranger to the podium. Her Paralympic career has spanned nearly two decades, during which she has won 10 medals.

to win a Paralympic medal in his or her native country. The same year, she also became the first Aboriginal athlete inducted into the Canadian Disability Hall of Fame.

Early Years

Bourgonje was born in 1962 and grew up in the small community of Porcupine Plain, Saskatchewan. She is of **Métis** ancestry. Her mother, Sheila, worked in the Porcupine Plain Credit Union, a financial institution owned and operated by its members. Her father, Jack, was an electrician who worked at various jobs.

Bourgonje loved sports and knew she wanted to be an athlete from an early age. Her family went cross-country skiing, and she was active in many different sports. In elementary school, Bourgonje played hockey with her older brother and cousins. When she got older, she played junior tackle football with the same cousins. At school, she was always the first student out the door to play soccer. Bourgonje also competed in other sports, including basketball, volleyball, badminton, and track and field.

In high school, Bourgonje was known as a star athlete. She continued to play basketball, volleyball, and badminton, and she twice competed nationally in cross-country running. Her goal was to become a physical education teacher when she grew up.

> **"** *Just because you are in a wheelchair, it doesn't change who you are. You find out how to adjust, you learn to adapt and make it work.* **"**

In the long-distance races for cross-country skiing at the Paralympic Winter Games, athletes are divided into several categories. Bourgonje races in the sit-skiing category.

BORN Colette Bourgonje was born on January 17, 1962, in the city of Saskatoon, Saskatchewan.

FAMILY Bourgonje grew up in the small town of Porcupine Plain, Saskatchewan, where she was raised by her parents. She has a sister, Yvette, and two brothers, Everett and Trevett.

EDUCATION In 1984, Bourgonje received a Bachelor of Science degree in physical education from the University of Saskatchewan. She earned a Bachelor of Education degree in 1985.

CAREER Between 1992 and 2010, Bourgonje competed in nine Paralympic Games, both Winter and Summer.

Developing Skills

Bourgonje had worked hard through high school to develop the athletic skills needed to become a top competitor. When she was 18, she faced new challenges when she was in a car accident that left her paralyzed from the waist down. She had to adjust to many changes and learn how to get around in a wheelchair.

Canada's first medal of the 2010 Paralympic Games was won by Bourgonje on Day 3 of the Games. She placed second in the women's sit-ski cross-country event.

This was a difficult time for Bourgonje, but she did not give up on her dreams. She entered the University of Saskatchewan, and four years later, she became the first student in a wheelchair to graduate from the university's program in physical education.

"I couldn't have written my life. My life has been quite a journey. Age is nothing, attitude is everything."

The Path to Success

Although Bourgonje could no longer compete in all of the sports she had once excelled in, she was committed to being an athlete. While at university, Bourgonje took up the sport of wheelchair racing, and in 1984, she competed in her first 10-kilometre race. She was not happy with the result, so she began to train hard, and her times improved. In 1992, she went to the Paralympic Summer Games for the first time. Bourgonje won two bronze medals in wheelchair racing.

Meanwhile, in 1991, she had started to learn the sport of sit-ski racing. Bourgonje trained five or six times a week. In 1992, she entered sit-ski races at the Winter Paralympics in Tignes and Albertville, France. Since then, Bourgonje has taken part in both Summer and Winter Paralympics, winning silver and bronze medals in both types of games.

Bourgonje was given a special honour at the 2010 Paralympics. She received the Whang Young Dai Achievement Award, given to Paralympic athletes who inspire other people. She now works with the organization Sask Sport to develop skiing programs for people with physical disabilities.

Accomplishments

1992 Bourgonje wins two bronze medals in wheelchair racing at the Paralympic Summer Games in Barcelona, Spain.

1996 At the Paralympic Summer Games, held in Atlanta, Georgia, Bourgonje wins two additional bronze medals in wheelchair racing.

1998 She is inducted into the Saskatoon Sport Hall of Fame after winning two silver medals in sit-skiing at the Paralympic Winter Games, held in Nagano, Japan.

2006 Bourgonje wins two more bronze medals in sit-skiing at the Paralympic Winter Games in Turin, Italy.

2010 At the Paralympic Winter Games, held in Vancouver, British Columbia, she wins a silver and a bronze medal in sit-skiing.

2011 Bourgonje is awarded the gold medal in the sit-ski distance race at the Para-Nordic World Championships, held in Khanty-Mansiysk, Russia.

Olympic Kayaker
Alwyn Morris

Alwyn Morris was a **kayaker** who in 1984 became the first Canadian Aboriginal athlete to win a gold medal at the Olympic Games. When Morris was 12 years old, he had promised his grandfather that he would be an Olympian. He went even farther than that, becoming an Olympic champion. Morris also became the third Aboriginal athlete to win a gold medal in the history of the Olympics. The others were Jim Thorpe and Billy Mills from the United States. Morris had trained for years in order to be successful.

Hugh Fisher and Alwyn Morris were teammates for six years. They competed in K2 events at the 1984 and 1988 Summer Olympics. K2 is a code used to define the race, where K stands for kayak and 2 represents the number of people in each boat.

Personal Profile

Morris now speaks with young people across Canada. He helped create the Alwyn Morris Education and Athletic Foundation to help young people. He also worked to establish the Aboriginal Sport Circle.

Early Years

Alwyn Morris was born in 1957 on the Kahnawake reserve, which is located on the shore of the St. Lawrence River, near Montreal, Quebec. Morris is a Mohawk. The Mohawks are one of the Six Nations of the Iroquois Confederacy.

Morris lived with his mother, Helen, and stepfather, Jim Montour. When he was growing up, he was close to his grandparents, Angela and Tom Morris. After his grandfather became ill, Morris moved in with his grandparents so that he could help them out.

The children on the reserve were active. They went swimming and played hockey and baseball. When he was young, Morris also wanted to play lacrosse, but he was told that he was too small.

> **"** *I raised the feather [during the Olympic medal ceremony] to . . . identify the fact that I was a Mohawk person, and I was very proud of that aspect; of being able to share that experience of being an Aboriginal person, share the aspect of my grandfather, and the honour that I wanted to bestow on him.* **"**

A rowing club opened on the Kahnawake reserve when Morris was 14. The club could be used by both recreational and competitive rowers. Morris was curious about kayaking but did not know much about it, so he decided to try it out. After a few mishaps landed him in the water, he decided that kayaking was fun and began training in earnest.

BORN Alwyn Morris was born on November 22, 1957, on the Kahnawake reserve near Montreal, Quebec.

FAMILY Morris grew up on the Kahnawake reserve, with his mother and stepfather. His grandparents, Tom and Angela Morris, helped raise him. Today, Morris is the father of two children.

EDUCATION He attended Douglas College and Simon Fraser University, both in British Columbia.

CAREER Morris began competing in kayaking in the 1970s. After the 1984 Olympics, he worked with drug and alcohol prevention groups. Today, he is involved with several sports organizations.

"The time and energy I dedicated to training and competing in the Olympics easily carried over into my career in government, business and as an Aboriginal ambassador. I knew that with enough hard work and dedication I could achieve nearly anything I set my mind to. . . ."

Developing Skills

Morris worked and practised hard. He began competing at the provincial and then the national level. In 1977, he won the Canadian junior national championships, but he wanted to further develop his skills and become even better. He knew that to keep improving, he needed to train with the best.

Morris decided to move to Burnaby, British Columbia, thousands of kilometres away from his home. A top-level racing and training site had recently been built on Burnaby Lake, and other serious kayakers were working there. It was difficult for Morris to leave his friends and family behind, but he knew he had to do so to succeed.

The Path to Success

Morris wanted to compete in the 1980 Summer Olympics, but Canada decided not to take part in the Olympics that year. Morris had to put his Olympic dream on hold for four years. Meanwhile, in Burnaby, he met another kayaker named Hugh Fisher. They decided to become a **doubles** team. They set their sights on the 1984 Olympics, which were going to be held in Los Angeles, California.

Morris and Fisher went to Europe to train as hard as they could. They won a silver medal at the 1982 World Championships. The following year, they won a bronze medal at the World Championships.

Their greatest achievement came at the 1984 Summer Olympics. There, Morris and Fisher won the gold medal in the men's 1,000-metre doubles kayak race, coming from behind to win. They also won the bronze medal in the 500-metre race. When he received the gold medal, Morris waved an eagle feather above his head. He did it for his grandfather, who had passed away in 1980.

After the Olympics, Morris was named Ambassador of Youth in Canada. As ambassador, he visited First Nations communities across Canada to encourage young people to pursue their dreams. He was also named to the Order of Canada, which is one of the highest honours in the country.

Morris has been active in efforts to reduce the problems of alcohol and drug abuse. As the national spokesperson for PRIDE, the Parents Resource Institute on Drug Education, he has worked with First Nations communities across Canada to promote prevention programs for drugs and alcohol.

Accomplishments

1977 Morris becomes the Canadian junior national champion in men's singles kayak racing. He also receives the Tom Longboat Award.

1982 With teammate Hugh Fisher, Morris wins a silver medal at the kayaking World Championships.

1983 Again racing with Fisher, he wins a bronze medal at the kayaking World Championships.

1984 At the Summer Olympic Games in Los Angeles, California, Morris and Fisher win a gold medal and a bronze medal. That year, Morris also receives the Tom Longboat Award for the second time.

1996 Morris receives the National Aboriginal Achievement Award for Sports.

2000 For their achievements, Morris and Fisher are inducted into the Canadian Sports Hall of Fame.

Prior to the 2010 Vancouver Olympics, the Olympic flame took a 45,000-kilometre journey across the country that lasted for 106 days. Morris carried the flame through the Kahnawake Mohawk reserve.

Wheelchair Basketball Player
Richard Peter

Richard Peter is one of the best wheelchair basketball players in the world. He has been a member of the Canadian men's wheelchair basketball team since 1994 and has won many gold medals during his long career. Peter has inspired many people, who admire the time and effort he devoted to joining the national team and becoming a successful athlete. Peter has also played an important role in promoting wheelchair sports and speaking out about the need to provide funding for Aboriginal athletes.

Personal Profile

As part of Canada's wheelchair basketball team, Peter played against Australia in the gold medal game of the 2004 Paralympics in Athens, Greece. Canada won the game, 70–53.

Peter was one of only two Canadian Aboriginal athletes at the 2008 Paralympic Games, serving as an important role model for young Aboriginal people.

People give up on their dreams because there are obstacles, but sometimes you have to get out there and overcome the obstacles and reach for the star that's right in front of you.

Early Years

Richard Peter was born in 1972 in Duncan, British Columbia, which is located on Vancouver Island. He grew up there with his parents, Gloria and Leonard, and three younger brothers and sisters, Shelley, William, and Violet. Peter grew up in a family whose members loved sports and participated in many activities. He never had a problem finding playmates. His parents had many brothers and sisters, and Peter had many cousins. His days were filled with playing and visiting with his cousins and his grandparents. Peter is a member of the **Cowichan** people.

When Peter was four years old, he was hit by a school bus. The accident left him paralyzed from the waist down. At first, Peter found life difficult in Duncan, since going to school and even visiting with family was challenging in a wheelchair. Buildings in Duncan, as in many towns at the time, were not wheelchair accessible.

Even though he was in a wheelchair, however, he led an active life. He credits his parents with encouraging him to be involved in sports and to enjoy himself. He often joined his friends in games of hockey, softball, and football. Through sports, Peter learned how to be a good teammate and also discovered that he liked playing with a team. As he later stated, "Being part of a team and working together towards a common goal has been a defining aspect of my life."

BORN Richard Peter was born on September 10, 1972, in Duncan, on Vancouver Island in British Columbia.

FAMILY Peter grew up with his parents and his brother and sisters. In 2005, he married Marni Abbott, a former member of the Canadian women's wheelchair basketball team.

EDUCATION Peter attended public school in Duncan. In school, he enjoyed mathematics, physical education, woodworking, computers, and English.

CAREER He has been a member of the Canadian men's wheelchair basketball team since 1994. He has also played for professional teams in Italy and Germany.

" . . . I'm very proud of being First Nations, and I think I show others in my community that whatever the obstacle, you can get to the top with a lot of hard work. "

Developing Skills

In 1987, a group of special athletes visited Peter's school. They were part of a wheelchair basketball team from Victoria, British Columbia. Peter played basketball with them in front of the school.

The team members had special wheelchairs that were designed for sports. Peter had a much heavier chair that was harder to move around quickly. Even so, he played very well. He was so determined that the team invited him to train with them. He began going to Victoria every weekend to work out with the team.

The Path to Success

It took Peter years of training and hard work to make the difficult leap from amateur competition to the national team. His family, community, and the Cowichan Tribes provided money to help. Peter says that one of the biggest challenges he faced as a First Nations athlete was getting financial support and transportation. Wheelchair basketball can be an expensive sport, since sports wheelchairs cost thousands of dollars.

In 1994, Peter moved to Vancouver for more training opportunities. There, he could learn wheelchair basketball from top-level athletes. He worked very hard and made the Canadian national team. Teammates gave Peter the nickname "Little Bear." As he gained

Peter has helped Team Canada reach much success on the court, including their gold medal victory at the 2000 Paralympic Summer Games.

more experience on the team, this nickname was changed to just "Bear."

In 1996, Peter went to his first Paralympic Summer Games, in Atlanta, Georgia. Although the Canadian team did not win a medal, Peter learned from this experience. Four years later, the team went to the Summer Paralympics again, this time in Sydney, Australia, where they won the gold medal. Then, at the 2004 Paralympics, in Athens, Greece, the Canadians did not lose a single game and won another gold medal. In 2008, they won a silver medal at the Paralympics in Beijing, China.

Peter has played in the world championships many times. As a member of Team Canada, he helped bring home bronze medals in 1994, 1998, and 2002, and the gold medal in 2006. He also plays with Team BC in Canada and has led the team to several national championships.

Accomplishments

2000 Peter and the Canadian men's wheelchair basketball team win the gold medal at the Paralympic Summer Games, in Sydney, Australia. Peter also receives the Tom Longboat Award.

2004 Peter and the Canadian team again win the gold medal at the Paralympic Games, in Athens, Greece. He receives his second Tom Longboat Award.

2007 He receives the Canadian Wheelchair Sports Athlete of the Year Award.

2008 Peter and the Canadian team win the silver medal at the Paralympic Games, in Beijing, China.

2010 He is inducted into the British Columbia Sports Hall of Fame.

2012 Peter receives the National Aboriginal Achievement Award.

Monica Pinette

Monica Pinette is a two-time Olympian and has won two medals at the **Pan American Games**. She is also a three-time Canadian champion in the sport of modern pentathlon. This challenging sport includes five events. Pentathlon competitors must shoot, fence, swim, run, and ride horses in the course of a single day. To be successful in modern pentathlon, athletes need strength, endurance, and skill. Pinette has proved that she has all three of these qualities.

At the 2004 Olympics, Pinette and her teammate, Kara Grant, were the first Canadian women ever to compete in modern pentathlon at the Olympics. Pinette was also the

Pinette was riding horses at a young age. The riding portion of the pentathlon is considered her strongest event.

Personal Profile

only Aboriginal athlete from Canada at the Games. To show her pride, she wore a colorful Métis sash at the closing ceremonies. Four years later, at the 2008 Olympics, she was again the only Aboriginal Canadian athlete.

Early Years

Monica Pinette was born in 1977 in British Columbia. She grew up on a small farm in Langley, not far from Vancouver. There, her father, Roger, owns a nursery, specializing in water gardens. Her mother, Gilian, breeds horses. Pinette's family was always very involved with horses.

Pinette was active from a very early age. She began riding horses when she was very young. In fact, Pinette jokes that she has been riding horses since before she was born.

In 1987, Pinette joined the Langley Pony Club, where she continued to ride. Pony Clubs are for young people who are interested in riding and

"*I think in recent years there's been more attention paid to Aboriginals . . . . it just became something to be proud of instead of something to be ashamed of.*"

caring for ponies and horses. At the Pony Club, Pinette enjoyed taking part in rallies, which are competitions often made up of different riding and jumping events. She also competed in the Prince Philip Games, a team competition for Pony Clubs around the world. Pinette loved being in the Pony Club. It gave her a chance to compete and be on a team.

Even with her busy training schedule, Pinette maintained contact with Pony Clubs by giving riding lessons and testing young riders.

BORN Monica Pinette was born on February 5, 1977, in the city of Vancouver, British Columbia.

FAMILY Pinette's father, Roger, is Métis. Her mother, Gilian, is from Kenya. Pinette has an older brother named Jeremy. Pinette is married. She and her husband, Philipp Waeffler, have one child.

EDUCATION Pinette received a Bachelor of Arts degree in English and writing from the University of Victoria. She also has a diploma in journalism from the Western Academy of Photography in Victoria.

CAREER Pinette competed in the modern pentathlon at the 2004 and 2008 Olympics. She has also competed in other international events.

"When I decided to try [modern pentathlon] I thought 'I'm already really good at one of these sports. I only have to learn four more.'"

Developing Skills

As a member of the Langley Pony Club, Pinette was introduced to many sports related to horseback riding. One of these sports was tetrathlon, which involves riding, running, swimming, and shooting. By the time she was a teenager, she was also giving riding lessons and working as a groom at a race course in Vancouver. She took up the sport of pentathlon, which is similar to tetrathlon, when she was 20.

In 2001, Pinette travelled with the Canadian team to Mexico City, Mexico. There, she competed in modern pentathlon for the first time. She had so much fun that she decided to continue in the sport. The following year, she went to the World Championships for the first time and came in 54th. This was a good result since she had been competing for less than a year.

The Path to Success

While training, Pinette lived in a house in Victoria, British Columbia, that was nicknamed the "pentathlon house," since many other athletes lived there. She had to juggle her athletic and educational activities, since she was also attending the University of Victoria. To train and compete, Pinette had to travel a great deal. She worked hard so that she could do well in her sport. In 2003, she won the Canadian National Pentathlon Championship. Pinette also entered the Pan American Games for the first time in 2003, placing an impressive

Pinette visited the Aboriginal Sport Gallery at the BC Sports Hall of Fame after it opened in June 2008. The gallery honours the contributions of Aboriginal athletes to the sport heritage of British Columbia.

seventh. Even though she was doing well as a pentathlete, Pinette still had to struggle. She needed money to continue to train. She was helped by her family, her friends, the Canadian Modern Pentathlon Federation, and several private companies.

Pinette moved to Switzerland, where pentathlon is more popular and there are greater training opportunities. She worked harder than ever, and her efforts brought her more international success. In 2004, she took part in her first Olympic Games, in Athens, Greece. She finished 13th, which was Canada's best placing ever in pentathlon. Pinette continued to compete and do well. In 2006, she won the Canadian championship and a gold medal at an international competition in Mexico. She won the Canadian championship again in 2007, as well as a silver medal at the Pan American Games. At the 2008 Olympics, in Beijing, China, Pinette placed 27th. After the Olympics, Pinette coached the Canadian junior team at the 2009 World Championships in Taiwan.

Accomplishments

2003 Pinette wins the Canadian national championship in modern pentathlon.

2004 Pinette takes part in the Olympics in Athens, Greece. She places 13th.

2006 She again wins the Canadian championship. She then wins the gold medal at an international competition in Mexico City, Mexico.

2007 Pinette wins the Canadian championship. She also wins the silver medal at the Pan American Games.

2008 Pinette again represents Canada at the Olympic Games, in Beijing, China.

2010 She receives the National Aboriginal Achievement Award.

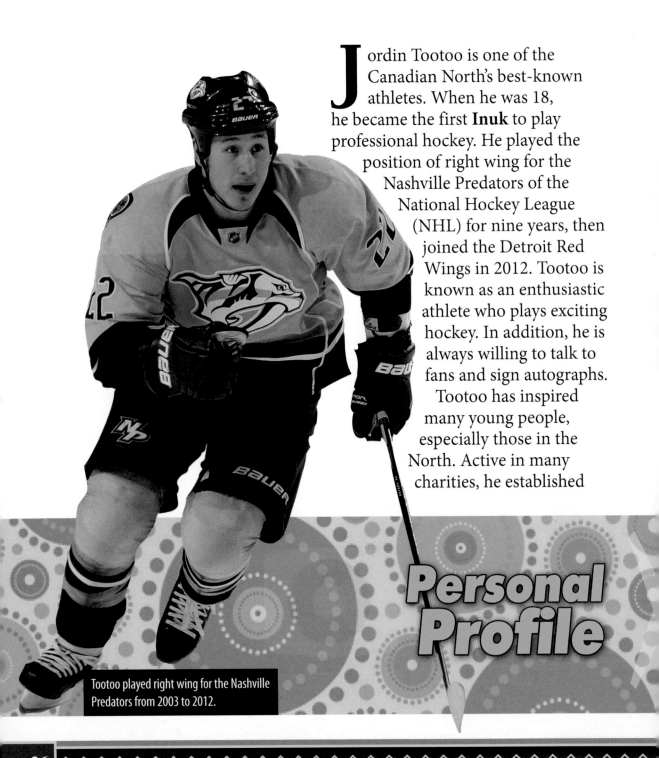

Hockey Player
Jordin Tootoo

Jordin Tootoo is one of the Canadian North's best-known athletes. When he was 18, he became the first **Inuk** to play professional hockey. He played the position of right wing for the Nashville Predators of the National Hockey League (NHL) for nine years, then joined the Detroit Red Wings in 2012. Tootoo is known as an enthusiastic athlete who plays exciting hockey. In addition, he is always willing to talk to fans and sign autographs. Tootoo has inspired many young people, especially those in the North. Active in many charities, he established

Tootoo played right wing for the Nashville Predators from 2003 to 2012.

Personal Profile

the Team Tootoo Fund to encourage his fans to donate money to nonprofit organizations that are important to him. He volunteers at holiday toy drives, donates equipment to youth hockey leagues, and also runs hockey clinics that teach playing skills to young athletes. In northern communities, Tootoo is seen as a role model, encouraging students to stay in school.

Early Years

Jordin Tootoo was born in 1983. He grew up in the small northern community of Rankin Inlet, Nunavut, which is located on the northwest shore of Hudson Bay. His father, Barney, is an Inuk, while his mother, Rose, is of Ukrainian descent. Tootoo's parents encouraged him to excel in school and sports. His father was an important role model for Tootoo. Before becoming a plumber in Rankin Inlet, Barney had played hockey in the **minor leagues**, and he wanted Tootoo and his older brother, Terence, to learn

the sport, too. Tootoo first put on skates at the age of two, and by the age of five, he was playing hockey.

> **"** *Follow your dreams, stay in school, and keep working hard every day.* **"**

Barney acted as Tootoo's first coach. In addition to teaching him hockey skills, he taught Tootoo to stand up for himself and to be a tough player. Tootoo often played with boys who were older than him, and he learned not to let bigger boys intimidate him. Tootoo and his brother played hockey for hours every day on natural ice as well as Rankin Inlet's indoor rink.

When not playing hockey, Tootoo enjoys watching basketball. His other hobbies include fishing, hunting, and golf.

BORN Jordin John Kudluk Tootoo was born on February 2, 1983, in the town of Churchill, Manitoba.

FAMILY Tootoo was raised by his parents, Rose and Barney. Tootoo had an older brother, named Terence, and he has a sister, named Corinne.

EDUCATION Tootoo went to school in Rankin Inlet, Nunavut.

CAREER Tootoo played for the OCN Blizzard team in the Manitoba Junior Hockey League and then for the Brandon Wheat Kings. In 2003, he joined the Nashville Predators of the NHL.

> *"There [are] a lot of positive things to look forward to in life. You've got to make that first step and you've got to fight through it."*

Developing Skills

When Tootoo was 14, he made the difficult decision to leave his community in order to improve his hockey skills. At first, he played for the OCN Blizzard, a junior-league hockey team in The Pas, Manitoba. Then, he moved on to Brandon, Manitoba, where he played for the Brandon Wheat Kings. Tootoo was one of the most popular players on the team. Still, it was hard for him to be away from home. Manitoba was very different from Nunavut, and he had a demanding schedule of daily hockey practice, games, school, and homework. To keep his spirits up, his mother sent him packages of Arctic foods, such as caribou and whale meat.

Tootoo's aggressive style of play attracted the attention of **scouts** from the NHL. Even before he turned 18, there were rumours that he would be **drafted** by an NHL team. The rumours turned out to be true. In 2001, he was drafted by the Nashville Predators, a team that plays in Nashville, Tennessee. Until Tootoo was ready to move up to the NHL, he continued playing for the Wheat Kings.

The Path to Success

A tragedy happened in 2002. Tootoo's brother, Terence, who also played for the Wheat Kings, committed suicide. Tootoo had to deal with his grief after this event, and Terence was never far from his mind. He dedicated the season to Terence's memory and wrote

Tootoo's favourite hockey moment was playing for Team Canada at the 2003 World Junior Championships. He scored only one goal, but he was one of the most popular players in the tournament.

Terence's name on his hockey sticks. Unfortunately, Tootoo did something else to try to deal with the tragedy. He turned to alcohol to relieve the pain of losing his brother.

Tootoo also dedicated himself to becoming an NHL player. In 2003, the Predators gave him an NHL **contract**. On October 9, 2003, with approximately 40 of his friends and family cheering him on, waving flags and banners, he played his first game in the NHL. Tootoo became known in the NHL as a fearless player who was ready to fight. He knew, though, that he had to solve his personal problems. With the support and encouragement of his coach and team, in late 2010, Tootoo entered a special NHL program to deal with his drinking problem. He completed the program and rejoined the Predators a few months later. In 2012, Tootoo signed a new contract to play for Detroit. The Red Wings felt they needed an aggressive player such as Tootoo to help them win more games.

Accomplishments

1998–1999 Tootoo is named **Rookie** of the Year for the OCN Blizzard.

2001 He is drafted by the Nashville Predators of the National Hockey League (NHL).

2002 Tootoo receives the National Aboriginal Achievement Youth Award. In addition, he receives the Tom Longboat Award.

2003 As a member of Team Canada, Tootoo wins a silver medal at the World Junior Championships. Months later, he plays in his first NHL game with the Predators.

2012 Tootoo signs a new contract to play for the NHL's Detroit Red Wings.

Write a Biography

All of the parts of a biography work together to tell the story of a person's life. Find out how these elements combine by writing a biography. Begin by choosing a person whose story fascinates you. You will have to research the person's life by using library books and reliable websites. You can also email the person or write him or her a letter. The person might agree to answer your questions directly.

Use a concept web, such as the one below, to guide you in writing the biography. Answer each of the questions listed using the information you have gathered. Each heading on the concept web will form an important part of the person's story.

Parts of a Biography

Early Life

Where and when was the person born?

What is known about the person's family and friends?

Did the person grow up in unusual circumstances?

Growing Up

Who had the most influence on the person?

Did he or she receive assistance from others?

Did the person have a positive attitude?

Developing Skills

What was the person's education?

What was the person's first job or work experience?

What obstacles did the person overcome?

Early Achievements

What was the person's most important early success?

What processes does this person use in his or her work?

Which of the person's traits were most helpful in his or her work?

Person Today

Has the person received awards or recognition for accomplishments?

What is the person's life's work?

How have the person's accomplishments served others?

Internet Resources

Aboriginal Canada Portal

This website is a partnership between the Canadian government and the Aboriginal community. There are many links to topics related to Aboriginal sports.

WEBSITE: www.aboriginalcanada.gc.ca/acp/site.nsf/eng/ao26713.html

The Aboriginal Circle

The Aboriginal Circle provides information on programs and events, including sports, for First Nations, Métis, and Inuit people throughout Canada.

WEBSITE: www.aboriginalcircle.com/home

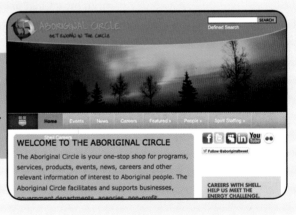

Virtual Museum of Canada

The website of the museum includes pages devoted to an exhibit exploring North American indigenous games. Find out about the Sacred Run, lacrosse, and traditional Métis and Inuit games.

WEBSITE: www.museevirtuel-virtualmuseum.ca/sgc-cms/expositions-exhibitions/traditions/English/index.html

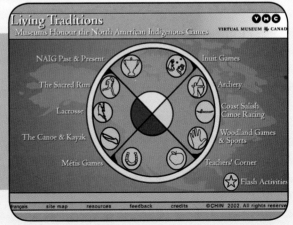

Glossary

Aboriginal: a term that refers to the First Nations, Métis, and Inuit peoples of Canada

Aboriginal Sport Circle: a national Canadian organization that supports sports among the Aboriginal Peoples

biathlon: a sport that combines both cross-country skiing and target shooting

contract: an agreement between two people or groups that makes it necessary to perform a specific action or actions

Cowichan: a First Nations people traditionally located in British Columbia

doubles: in sports, a team made up of two people

drafted: chosen by a sports team

indigenous: referring to the culture of a group of people originally living in an area

Inuk: a person who is a member of the Inuit, a group of people who have traditionally lived in Canada's Arctic regions

Iroquois Confederacy: an association made up of several different indigenous groups in North America

kayaker: someone who paddles a kayak, a boat that is similar to a canoe

lacrosse: a game in which a long-handled stick with a pouch is used to catch and throw a ball

marathon: a long-distance race that is 42.2 kilometres (26 miles, 385 yards) long

Métis: a person who is of mixed Aboriginal and European descent

minor leagues: professional teams below the highest level

Olympic Games: games held every four years in the winter and summer in which athletes from the around the world compete in a variety of sports

Pan American Games: games held every four years in which people from the Americas compete in a variety of sports

reserve: land set aside by the federal government for the use and occupancy of a First Nations group

rookie: a player in his first year with a team or league

scouts: people who observe athletes to see if they should be hired by teams

sit-ski: a specially made chair, with seat belts and straps, that is attached to one or two skis, so that people with physical disabilities affecting the lower part of their body can ski

stereotypes: images, often negative, about a person or group

Index